THE ART OF BROMOIL
CENTENARY
2007

THE BROMOIL CIRCLE OF GREAT BRITAIN

Sam Weller – Sunny Mead of Dedham (23x27cm)

THE ART OF BROMOIL
CENTENARY
2007

THE BROMOIL CIRCLE OF GREAT BRITAIN
FOUNDED BY SAM WELLER 1931

Published by **The Bromoil Circle of Great Britain** 2007

ISBN: 978-0-9557199-0-5

Printed: ALDINE PRINT LTD., Malvern, WR14 3NB – info@aldineprint.co.uk

CONTENTS

ACKNOWLEDGEMENTS

As President of The Bromoil Circle of Great Britain it is my privilege and it gives me great pleasure to convey the Society's sincerest thanks to everyone involved in bringing "The Art of Bromoil Centenary - 2007" to fruition, both for their contributions to the book and for their work.

Acknowledgement is also due to the members of the past whose many images, owned by the Circle and included here, have been inspirational, helping to take the fascinating Art of Bromoil into the 21st century against all odds.

A substantial grant was awarded by the Heritage Lottery Fund to the Circle in March 2007. The Society would like to thank the Heritage Lottery Fund for the financial support which has enabled it to realise, besides the book, an all embracing Centenary Project with the aim of ensuring the survival of the process.

It is also hoped that the book will bring much pleasure to readers and owners and act, perhaps, for some as a catalyst to become a practising bromoilist of the future.

Finally, I would like to offer here a brief description of the layout of the images. Nos. 1- 23 represent the work of past Presidents of the Society, covering the years 1931-2000. The next, Nos. 24 - 81 are images by the present day members, and Nos. 82 - 100 are prints by past members selected from the Circle's Permanent Collection.

Maija McDougal *FRPS*
President
The Bromoil Circle of Great Britain

Pathway to the Bromoil Process

Accidental discoveries and scientific experiments, both, gave birth to photography around the middle of the 19th century. The players in this field were numerous. Each contribution paved the way towards developing and perfecting the new medium.

When browsing through the literature on the history of photography, it may come as a surprise to read that the discovery of the chemical Silver Salts being light sensitive was made as early as 1725, a full century before the photographers Henry Fox Talbot and Louis Daguerre presented the results of their experiments to the world.

It had been observed, all along with great concern, that silver based photographic images, under prolonged exposure to light, became unstable. The images had the tendency to fade. To solve the problem, experiments were conducted to replace the fugitive silver with more stable substances. Pure pigments in powder form, water-colours, painters' oils and printers' inks became the substitutes.

These experiments led, intentionally or unintentionally, to the invention and the use of the so called Pigment or Control Processes, now referred to as Alternative Printing Processes. The main ones are: Carbon, Gum, Oil and Bromoil. In all these printing techniques, to reveal the images, the above mentioned artists' materials were used in combination with the chemicals used in conventional photography.

Before describing the Alternative Printing Processes, several discoveries of the 1830s and 1850s will have to be mentioned here - first, Fox Talbot's invention of the negative and secondly, the discovery made by the Scotsman, Mongo Ponton, that the chemical Bichromate (now referred to as Dichromate) was sensitive to light. The next of importance was, again, Fox Talbot's discovery in 1850 that colloids, such as gelatine, gum and albumen, would harden when mixed with Dichromate and exposed to light. Colloids proved to be the most suitable substances in which the light sensitive chemicals and pigments could be suspended. Being viscous, it was comparatively easy to coat papers or other surfaces used for the printing processes. Thus, the negative, the chemical Dichromate and colloids became the indispensable materials to the workers in the Control Processes.

As is well known, during the second half of the 19th century, photographers were not preoccupied with chemistry alone. The new medium, almost from the start, could not escape being compared with the long established visual arts, painting in particular. Passionate discussions, pros and cons, were conducted at great length, mainly comparing a photograph, an image obtained using a mechanical apparatus, with a painting, the artistically created image, in respect to their inherent aesthetic values.

The first deliberate and controlled manipulations in photography were practised by David Octavius Hill and Robert Adamson as early as 1840. To create certain effects, they were making alterations on the paper negatives with pencil markings where considered appropriate. Later, the practitioners of the Pigment Processes quickly realised the manipulative possibilities within their adopted medium. To enhance the image, extensive alterations were carried out by the available means.

An invention by the French photographer, Alfonso Louis Poitevin, was to become the first of the Alternative Printing Processes. He had successfully experimented with the pigment Carbon Black (soot) to replace the silver. In 1855 he patented what came to be known as the Carbon Process.

In this printing technique, the pigment Carbon Black was added to the sensitised colloid, a mixture of gelatine and Dichromate. A sheet of paper was coated with it. After being left to dry in the dark, it was exposed to light under a contact negative. Depending on the amount of light the paper had received through the negative, differential hardening of the pigment carrying gelatine was induced. After exposure, to develop the print, it was placed in a warm water bath. The unhardened colloid would dissolve and carry away with it most of the pigment particles, whereas the hardened gelatine would retain the pigment which then formed the image. Unfortunately the early Carbon prints lacked subtle half tones. With the later Carbon Transfer Process, this became possible, but we need not go into it here.

A few years later, in 1858, John Pouncy introduced the Gum Bichromate Printing Process. It was a variant to Carbon. In place of gelatine, Gum Arabic was used as the sensitised and pigment carrying colloid. This time, to develop the print, only a cold water bath was needed. As far as artistic manipulation was concerned, Gum printing was a more flexible process than Carbon. Local development could be carried out using sometimes soft brushes or by directing a fine jet of water onto a chosen area in the image. With these manipulations unwanted pigments could be removed at will.

In 1904, more or less 50 years after the contributions by Poitevin and Pouncy, G. H. Rawlins reintroduced the Carbon, but in a modified form. By then a paper, coated with gelatine only, had become available commercially. It was used in the earlier mentioned Carbon Transfer Process. Rawlins sensitised this paper with a Dichromate solution. The sensitised paper was exposed under a contact negative of available size. During the exposure, a latent image would form within the differentially hardened gelatine. After exposure the print was washed to remove the yellow Dichromate stain. Whilst the print remained moist, to reveal the image, Rawlins applied an oil based printing ink using a roller. As oil and water do not mix, the ink would be repelled from the softer, water swollen areas, but adhere to the more hardened gelatine. Thus the Oil Printing Process, the forerunner of Bromoil, was born.

Three years later, in 1907, a theoretical supposition was published by E. J. Wall. It stated that the gelatine in a silver based photograph could also be conditioned for pigmenting. However, the photograph would have to be treated with certain chemicals first. To remove the silver based image Copper Sulphate and for the differential hardening of the gelatine Potassium Dichromate solutions were used. These were to be the two main agents for conditioning the photographic paper to accept oil based printing inks. Wall stressed the advantage of this technique. The size of the print would no longer have to depend on the size of an available contact negative. The image could be enlarged directly on the silver based photographic paper of any size. To reveal the image, the inking could be carried out as for Oil printing.

In the same year, Wall's theory was put into practice by C. Welbourne Piper using the commercially available papers. For the treatment of the paper reliable chemical formulae were established. Sometimes small variations in the formula were recommended by other practitioners.

Soon brushes replaced the earlier inking tool, the roller. The use of brushes gave much greater control during inking. Textural variety could be introduced, depending on what kind of brushes were used. With the brushwork deliberate local tonal alterations could be achieved, offering further, almost unlimited scope for the interpretation of a subject. Thus, the Bromoil Printing Process, the most flexible of all the Control Processes, as bromoilists would like to believe, was born.

In the quest for further technical and artistic development, experimentation never ceased. In the Bormoil Process the use of coloured inks became popular. It has been stated that in 1911 Robert Demachy introduced the Bromoil Transfer Process. As printing presses became available, the transfer technique was practised by many workers and soon considered to be the ultimate goal.

From time to time attempts at introducing a "hybrid" have taken place. The best known, perhaps, are: Oleobrom, Bromaloid and Bromotype, the

originators being F. J. Shepherd, F. F. Renwick, G. L. Hawkins and B. Whiting respectively.

As can be expected, the last mentioned techniques were considered and recommended by the inventors as either superior, easier, more beautiful, more advantageous and so on, than the straightforward Bromoil and Oil Processes. Alas, these alternatives never gained a permanent footing, rising and falling like shooting stars in the sky. However, in the latter years, bromoilists, with inquisitive minds, have put these to the test again, but nothing more than that.

Lastly, a brief mention must be made of some of the companies involved in the manufacture of materials for the Bromoil Printing Process.

Griffin of Kingsway, London, marketed the paper for Rawlins' Oil Process. The Autotype Company was manufacturing the un-sized gelatine paper, mainly for the Carbon Transfer Process, but equally suitable for Oil printing. From C.Robertson & Co. and James Sinclair one could purchase brushes, pigments and the specially prepared inks. Sinclair was also selling the uniquely designed Bromoil Transfer press.

In the early days papers, in a great variety of colours, surface textures and gelatine swelling characteristics, came from: Ilford. Kodak, Agfa, Elliot & Sons of Barnet, Wellington & Ward Ltd. and Griffin, who named their paper amusingly "Pigmoil". Some papers were marketed exclusively as Bromoil papers - now a story of the past.

A special mention must be made of Kentmere & Co. of Staveley, Cumbria, U.K. Until very recently this company was still manufacturing at least one brand of paper that lent itself successfully to inking, but its future is uncertain.

During the last ten years, to find alternative materials, practitioners have been obliged to experiment with papers supplied by East European companies. Should the complete loss of suitable papers for the process happen in the future, bromoilists would have to prepare Art papers, of their own choice, by coating them with light sensitive emulsions. Who knows, this may just offer the elusive something extra one is always hoping and looking for in the creation of a Bromoil image.

Kirk Toft *LRPS*
Maija McDougal *FRPS*

A Short Past and Recent History of The Bromoil Circle of Great Britain

The Bromoil Circle Postal Club was formed by the late A. C. Weller, alias Sam Weller, of Pinner, London, in 1931, and later renamed as above. It took place during the period when Pigment Printing Processes had become popular amongst photographers.

The nature of the Bromoil Process and its intrinsic qualities lent itself admirably to the prevailing ideals in pictorial photography during the first half of the 20th century. Because of its popularity, it could not have been difficult for Sam Weller to gather under one roof a group of like minded practitioners. As they were scattered all over the country, the only way to achieve this was by forming a postal club. The aims of the Society were stipulated to facilitate the exchange of technical information, of individual working methods and ideas as well as the viewing and appraising of each others' images.

Sam Weller's first entry in "The Bromoil Circle Postal Club" accounts, "The Ledger and Cash Book", dated April 1931, records the names of 18 bromoilists. On the same page it also shows the annual subscription fee as being 5 shillings.

A system of 3 circulating boxes was adopted. With this number a membership to a maximum of 20 could be accommodated. Up to the mid 1980s, membership was mainly gained by recommendation and invitation. Aspiring to maintain the highest possible standards within the group, mostly experienced and established bromoilists seem to have been approached to become members of the Circle. Thus it does not come as a surprise to find that many of the outstanding bromoilists of the day had been recruited over the years. Amongst them were L. G. Hawkins, the author of "Pigment Printing", A. E. Brookes, the first President of Sutton Coldfield Photographic Society, Georgia Procter-Gregg and A. Barraclough, to mention but a few.

From the start, the running of the Circle must have been entrusted to a committee of 3, headed, no doubt, by Sam Weller. A brief reference to it can be found amongst the Circle's archival letters. A constitution must also have been formulated. Unfortunately both documentations have been lost. However, this has never impeded the uninterrupted activities of the Circle.

During the first 3 decades of the 20th century, Bromoil was to become one of the most popular of all the Pigment Printing Processes. Its extensive use lasted well into the 1960s and beyond. Evidence of the latter can be seen in an exhibition catalogue found, once again, in the Circle's archive. This was held in the Lewis Textile Museum and Art Gallery at Blackburn during February-March 1961. It records that in all 190 images were displayed by 63 artists. Of these 40 were bromoilists and amongst them no less than 20 were members of the Bromoil Circle. A commendable record for the Society.

Sam Weller's presidency lasted for over 30 years, to be precise, a full 32 years. Today his work can be found in the Permanent Collection, owned by the Circle, and amongst The Royal Photographic Society's collections. The latter are housed at the National Media Museum, Bradford.

Sadly, in November 1963, due to ill health, Sam Weller had to relinquish the post he had held for so long and was forced to retire from active participation in the Circle.

The Presidents to follow Sam Weller were: Godfrey Phillips 1964-1974, Frank Williams 1974-1981, Trevor Jones 1981-1987 and Gilbert Hooper 1987-2000, all outstanding bromoilists and as influential in the affairs of the Circle as Sam Weller had been.

As has already been mentioned, 3 postal boxes were used to circulate images and information. Members would receive the boxes at 8 week intervals. The prints, always mounted, were presented in folders. On these the author would enter technical data, the fellow members their comments and appraisals. Additionally a complementary note book, "The Folio", was provided where further information, pertaining to the process, and personal correspondence could be entered. This enabled the members to form closer partnerships and friendships.

Every submission would make 2 rounds so that the members could acquaint themselves with all the entries following their own. On these lines the Circle was jointly run by the serving President and the Hon. Secretary until 1998.

The post WW2 years saw great advancements and many changes in the photographic industry. An abundance of new materials and with it working techniques were introduced. Inevitably the materials which had been produced and used by bromoilists for many years were gradually withdrawn from the market. Bromoilists were losing one by one the most suitable and well tested papers, the specially prepared printing inks and some of the tools such as the traditional stag foot brushes.

Confronted with the losses and forced changes, alternatives had to be found and working techniques adapted accordingly. The Circle members were obliged to find and work with new materials. Their research and experimentation played an invaluable part in assuring the Art and Craft of bromoiling would survive and be passed on to future generations. As before, all new discoveries were passed on from member to member in the most generous manner via the circulating boxes.

During the 1970s and 80s the Circle experienced considerable fluctuation in membership numbers due to the difficulties arising from the changes in the industry. At times the membership fell to a mere dozen, sometimes even below. Thus grew the need to introduce and present the process to a wider audience if only to show it had not been abandoned completely and that it could still offer contemporary photographers a beautiful and unique medium for self expression. As well as being the custodians of the old, the members of the Circle became also the disseminators of all that was new.

To popularise the process the organising of demonstrations and workshops was intensified. These were offered and took place at photographic clubs, fairs and some colleges throughout the country. It proved to be most successful, attracting newcomers to the process. With it the demand for comprehensive technical information increased noticeably.

In 1998, in response to the demand, the Circle published a manual "An Introduction to Bromoil", compiled by the late Gilbert R. Hooper *FRPS*, Maija McDougal *FRPS* and Dennis Atherton *FRPS*. Soon afterwards a "Beginners' Kit" was made available by courtesy of Don Whitley *ARPS* of Eurolux, Shipley, North Yorkshire. The kit contained the most essential materials: suitable photographic paper, a brush, the chemicals for bleaching and tanning the bromide prints, etc.. It also included instructions, a copy of the above mentioned manual. The kit enabled anyone interested to explore the process without incurring great expense.

Well before 1998 it was felt a regular "Members' Meeting" should be introduced. The first had already been held at Shrewsbury in 1995. Since then these meetings have taken place annually at Shrewsbury, Shipley in North Yorkshire and Worcester. The meetings considerably widened the activities of the Circle. The face to face gatherings opened opportunities for live discussions, the presentation of personal portfolios and practical demonstrations. The latter have been conducted not only by the members, but also by a number of visiting artists, including the distinguished bromoilist, Gene Laughter, from the United States. Thus, by spreading its wings, the Society has become more than just a postal club.

One of the major undertakings for the Circle was the decision to stage exhibitions, always including a selection of images by the Society's past Presidents and members which are held in the Circle's Permanent Collection. The first of its kind took place at the Museum and Art Gallery of Falkirk in 1997. Further exhibitions followed, one in 2000 and the next in 2002, both at the "Design Exchange Gallery", Little Germany, Bradford. In 2007 the "Art of Bromoil - Centenary Exhibition" was shown extensively throughout the country, including Worcester, Halifax, Smethwick, with Nottingham and Banbury to follow.

With the general growth of interest in the Alternative Printing Processes during the last 2 decades, many Bromoil images by the members of the Circle have been presented in various publications, "Photo Art International", The Royal Photographic Society Pictorial Group magazine "Vision", and "The Amateur Photographer", amongst them.

Soon followed another innovation. A "Mentor's Scheme" was introduced offering a one to one partnership between an aspiring bromoilist and some of the most experienced members of the Circle. This facility was stipulated to last up to 12 months during which information and advice would be passed on by the Mentor to the enrolled participant with encouragement and general assessment on his or her submitted images.

A little later it was also decided that the Mentor's Scheme should replace the earlier mentioned conditions in gaining membership.

Due to all the above mention innovations, a pressing necessity presented itself, that is, for the Circle to form again an official body entrusted with the running of the expanding activities of the Society. In 1998 a new Constitution was formulated and a Management Committee established. The latter would embrace : 1)

The President, 2) The Past President, 3) The Hon. Secretary and Treasurer, 4) The Exhibition and Publicity Officer and 5) 2 Members without Portfolio.

Partially due to the Mentor's Scheme, applications for membership increased noticeably. At any time during the 12 months trial period the Mentor could submit a recommendation to the Management Committee for the Mentee to be offered membership. Alas, soon a shortage of vacancies arose. Not wanting to turn away those who had taken kindly to the process, the Circle was obliged to find a solution to this unexpected but welcome situation. Without making drastic changes to the established traditions, the only way out was to increase the number of circulating boxes, eventually to 5. With the new arrangements the membership could grow to a maximum of 30, which it did. The only disadvantage was the long wait before a print would complete the two rounds and could be retrieved by the owner.

It may be of interest to the reader to present here just two paragraphs from the Society's Constitution.

Paragraph 2: ...that it (the Circle) should exist for the furtherance of the Bromoil and related processes and function as a Postal Club. In addition it should endeavour to conserve and expand its Archive and Document Collection. Paragraph 3: ...it (the Circle) should aim to encourage the interchange of ideas, technical information, support education amongst bromoilists, historians and other researchers and the general public by suitable means.

As can be seen, the Society's main aims have remained identical to those intended by Sam Weller at its conception. At this point, the presented short history of The Bromoil Circle of Great Britain has made a full circle. The need to preserve this beautiful photographic printing process for posterity, however, has become much more acute today. The Circle is convinced that one of the best ways of ensuring that the process is not lost to future generations is by presenting to the public an informative and generously illustrated Centenary Book

Maija McDougal *FRPS*

An Introduction to Bromoil

Introduction

The Bromoil Process is a process whereby the silver image contained in a black and white photograph is replaced by an ink image. The process originated from the Oil Process, which was suggested in a patent dated 1855. It was in 1907 that C. Welbourne Piper worked out a formula for the Bromoil Process on a suggestion by E. J. Wall.

The method briefly is, that the silver image, contained in gelatine on a bromide print, is bleached away and at the same time the gelatine is hardened according to the amount of silver it contains. It is then fixed, washed and dried. To condition the gelatine for inking the print is re-soaked, removed from the dish and all surplus water wiped off. A greasy ink, such as lithographic ink, is then applied by brush. The ink is accepted where the gelatine has hardened (the shadow areas) but is rejected where the gelatine has swollen (the highlights). Thus the original silver image in the bromide print is changed into an ink image, which is far more permanent. By judicious application of the ink, the worker has great control over the final image. This process was much favoured by the pictorial workers of yesteryears and is now once more gaining in popularity.

How to make a Bromide Print.

The most frequently used bromide paper for the process is Kentmere Art Document, a fibre based paper. When starting the process, it is the easiest paper to use to achieve a reasonable result.

Prepare a normal bromide print, aiming for slightly veiled highlights and detail in the shadows. Leave a $^{1}/_{2}$" to 1" margin all round the image for handling purposes.

The developer I use to produce the image is the old D163 formula. All the chemical formulae are given at the end of this article.

For use, take 1 part of stock solution to 3 parts of water or as required to give the necessary contrast. When using a negative with a lot of contrast, the developer should be used weaker. Use all solutions at 68F (20C).

Having developed the print, fix it in a 10% plain Hypo bath for 5 minutes only. Wash the print thoroughly and dry it, usually over night.

Bleaching and tanning.

Soak the previously prepared print in clean water for 5 minutes at 68F. Remove from the water and blot off surplus water. Place the print in the bottom of a dish ready to receive the bleach-tan solution.

Use 1 part stock solution to 10 parts water at 68F.

Prepare sufficient bleach-tan solution to cover the bromide print in the bottom of the dish. Pour in the solution and keep rocking the dish for a full 10 minutes so that the tanning action is completed. Discard the bleach-tan solution after use.

Wash the print thoroughly to remove all traces of the bleach-tan solution and then fix it again in a 10% plain hypo solution, as before, for 5 minutes. Wash and dry thoroughly.

Applying ink to Matrix.

Materials required:

A dish in which to soak, also bleach-tan, the matrix.

Blotting paper and cotton wool.

A small dish or bowl to hold water for cleaning the matrix with the cotton wool.

A sheet of glass, larger than the matrix to be inked.

A sponge and a piece of chamois leather to remove surplus water.

An old handkerchief or piece of absorbent cloth to remove all water from the matrix.

Ink - the thickest litho ink available. I suggest Intaglio Black Lithographic Ink No.1803.

Brush - a cheap shaving or a decorator's brush trimmed to the shape of a stag's foot or horse's hoof. This can be achieved with a pair of scissors and finished off with an electric razor. (See illustration No. 2)

A 6" white glazed tile on which to mix and spread the ink

A small knife or palette knife to spread the ink with.

Artists' turpentine to thin the ink when necessary.

Method.

Take some of the ink, about the size of a small pea, on the tip of the knife and spread it in a patch on the tile. Mix well by spreading and removing it with the knife until there is a patch the size of about 1.5" by 2.5" ; holding the blade of the knife at about 45 degrees to the tile, gently remove the ink until there is only a thin layer left. Dab the brush on this patch of the ink so that only the tips of the bristles on the brush accept the ink. Now dab the brush on a clean part of

the tile. Build up this second patch of ink by dabbing repeatedly from the first patch. Only the tips of the brush should be charged with ink. When applying ink to the matrix, the brush should be used only from the second patch. (See illustration No. 1)

Soak the matrix for 3 minutes in clean water at 68F (20C). Remove from the dish and place it face down on the blotting paper. Remove surplus water from the back with the sponge.

Place the matrix face up on the sheet of glass and with the chamois leather gently remove the surplus water. Finish off by wiping with the old handkerchief or cloth, folded to form a pad, paying particular attention to the edges of the matrix. There should now be no signs of any water on the matrix or the glass sheet.

Apply the brush, previously charged with ink, to the matrix, starting at the top left and working down to the bottom with a dabbing dragging action, dab-drag-lift, dab-drag-lift. Return the brush to the top of the matrix and once more work to the bottom, working across the matrix to the right hand side. Charge the brush from the second patch of ink on the tile as and when necessary. (See illustration No. 3 and No. 6)

The matrix should be coated with a thin layer of ink, looking rather muddy, but with the image just showing through. Now change the action of the brush, dabbing the matrix without dragging. (See illustration No. 4) The image will start to clean up, becoming more prominent. Continue working with those two actions until no further progress seems to be made.

Put the brush to one side and with a swab of cotton wool, charged with water from the small dish or bowl, wipe over the image on the matrix. The image should now clean up and the highlight areas become more prominent and the contrast increased. Remove all surplus water again with the chamois leather and the handkerchief or cloth. Then resume inking again as before. The contrast should now build up. Be careful not to use too much ink. If the ink on the tile becomes dry, re-spread the surplus ink on the knife, as before, leaving a thin film on the tile. Recharge the brush, as and when required from the freshened patch. A more forceful dabbing will also increase contrast in the image. (See illustration No. 5)

As the image builds up, specific areas can be worked on. Shadow areas may require more ink, whilst the highlight areas may require lightening.

Brushes and equipment can be cleaned with lighter fuel, petrol or white spirit, but not turpentine substitute. If white spirit is used, leave the brushes for 24 hours to dry out.

Bromoil is a very personal process and success depends on cleanliness, attention to detail, patience and perseverance in the handling of the brush. Don't be disappointed if your first effort is not a masterpiece. Just persevere.

Every Bromoil is an original. No two can be exactly alike.

Gilbert R. Hooper *FRPS*

Editor's Note:
At the time of publishing this book, the manufacture of Kentmere Art Document paper has been discontinued. It is hoped that a replacement, suitable for the process, will come on the market at a future date.

Chemical Formulae.
Caution – Safety first!

Photographic chemicals can be dangerous if misused. Never let the chemicals come in contact with the skin. Recommended precautions: 1) when handling the chemicals wear a mask and protective gloves, 2) keep the chemicals in clearly labelled jars and bottles, 3) never smoke, eat or drink in the darkroom or wherever the chemicals are handled, 4) keep everything out of reach of children, 5) clean up spillage immediately, 6) if you get something in your eyes, wash immediately with plenty of water and seek medical advice immediately.

Kodak D-163 developer, stock solution:

Metol	– 2.3 g
Sodium Sulphite (anhydrous)	– 75.0 g
or Sodium Sulphite (crystals)	– 150.0 g
Hydroquinone	– 17.0 g
Sodium Carbonate (anhydrous)	– 65.0 g
or Sodium Carbonate (crystals)	– 175.0 g
Potassium Bromide	– 2.8 g
or Potassium Bromide (10% solution)	– 28 ml
Water to	– 1000 ml

Dissolve the chemicals in the order given. Use at 20C

Gilbert Hooper's Bleach / Tan formula, stock solution:

Copper Sulphate	– 25.0g
Potassium Bromide	– 25.0g
Potassium Dichromate	– 1.25g
Water to	– 400 ml

Fixative

Plain Hypo, 10% solution

Sodium Thiosulphate (crystals)	– 160.0 g

to 1000 ml (1 litre) of water.

Editor's note: Gilbert Hooper includes Sulphuric Acid in his Bleach / Tan solution. As this has proved not to be absolutely essential, for reasons of safety, it has been deleted from the formula here.

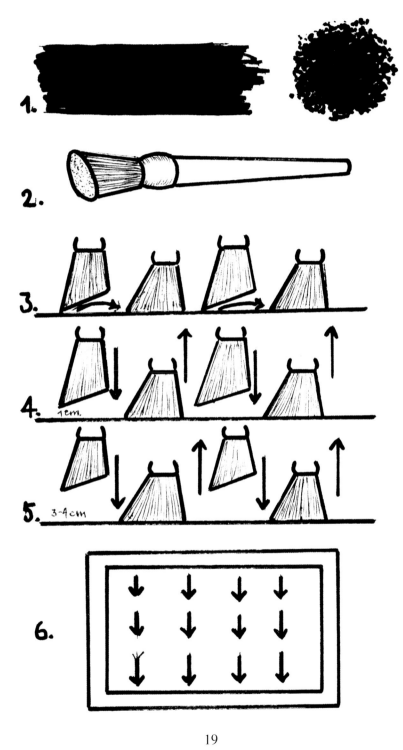

1.

2.

3.

4. 1cm

5. 3-4 cm

6.

19

The Bromoil Transfer Process

A Bromoil Transfer print is considered by many bromoilists to be the final and ultimate achievement in the Art of Bromoil.

The essential tool for making transfers, of course, is a printing press. Finding the specially designed pre-war press, by James A. Sinclair's company of London, or any other make, is almost impossible.

The most suitable alternative therefore would be an etching press, with which equally good results could be achieved. When contemplating purchasing one, the length of the roller and the width of the bed of the press should be considered. The size of these would determine the size of the receptor paper one could use and finally the image itself.

As far as the chemical treatment of the bromide print goes, the preparations for inking are the same as outlined in the chapter by Gilbert Hooper *FRPS*. There is, however, a slight difference regarding the inking. The matrix used for making a transfer should be inked with slightly greater contrast. It is important to keep the highlights very clean; the shadows, however, should be more heavily inked than in an ordinary Bromoil print. This is done because every pigment particle in the ink from the highlight areas will transfer onto the new support paper with ease, whereas only about 80%-90% from the shadows. Without sufficient contrast the transfer print will look dull and tonally degraded.

Once the inking has been completed, before a transfer is made, the matrix should be soaked for about 5 minutes. This will facilitate the release of the ink from the matrix. Before the pull is made, all surplus water must be removed from its surface. The receptor paper could be any good quality water-colour paper, preferably hot pressed (smooth), or makes of paper traditionally used by print makers.

The pressure of the press will have to be adjusted depending on the thickness of the pack that will be pulled through. The make up of the pack, referred to as the sandwich, may differ from one worker to another, but here is an example that has given good results. It is made up as follows: a thin card, larger than the receptor paper, forms the base. Placed on top of it is the water-colour paper and then, face down, the inked matrix, all in a staggered fashion. This pack of three is placed between two firm Acetate sheets. These should be glued together at one end, along the shorter edges. The sandwich is then placed on the bed of the press and pulled through slowly, without stopping and as smoothly as possible.

It is hoped that a satisfactory transfer with the first pull has been achieved showing all the desired detail and tonalities. As mentioned earlier, clean and sparkling highlights and deeply rich blacks are desirable. Should the image lack these elements, the print can be discarded and the matrix prepared for a second pull. For this, after a short soak, the matrix is re-inked. As before, attention should be paid to the highlights and shadows, particularly to the latter. These should receive plenty of ink.

The residual ink, that had remained on the matrix after the first pull, facilitates the release of the ink from the shadow areas when the pack is going through the press the second time.

The sandwich could be taken through the press in both directions to ensure more of the ink gets transferred. There is, however, some danger of losing sharpness in the print. The pack may have shifted out of register on the return journey.

A technique of several inkings and pulls from the same matrix onto the same support paper (multiple pulls) is practised by some workers. With the repeated soaking the expansion of the paper can vary. This will depend on the temperature of the water and the length of time of the soak. Good results would always depend on finding a reliable method of registration.

One way of achieving this is to draw 4 pencil lines on the back of the matrix after the first pull and before the matrix and the support paper are separated. The marks should be lengthened beyond the outer edges of the matrix onto the receptor paper.

Even more reliable results can be achieved when a damp matrix, prior to inking, is stretched by taking it through the press, also when a damp receptor paper is used. A close study of the behaviour of the papers used should be made. It is advisable to introduce standardisation in one's working methods thus minimizing variables to avoid unpredictability. It must be mentioned that the multiple pull technique is often used in colour work with great success.

And finally, one can only add that the end result, the Bromoil Transfer, liberated from all the materials used in photography, must be considered as a print in its truest sense and equal to any produced in the different printing processes. It has gained greater permanency than a Bromoil and an additional enhancement through the use of a beautiful hand made paper of one's choice.

Kenneth Hill *FRPS*

1. Sam Weller – April's Smiles (31x23cm)

2. Sam Weller – An Old Mill and Figure (34x24cm)

3. Sam Weller – The Fussy Tug (33x22cm)

4. Sam Weller – The Bucket (31x27cm)

5. Sam Weller – A Lonely Cottage (25x21cm)

6. Godfrey Phillips – Early Autumn Wind (17x15cm)

7. Godfrey Phillips – Scottish Landscape (22x14cm)

8. Godfrey Phillips – Sunlight Decorations (14x18cm)

9. Frank Williams – A Heavy Load (20x15cm)

31

10. Frank Williams – Basque Fishermen (13x19cm)

11. Frank Williams – The Sentinel (18x13cm)

12. Frank Williams – Street at Brigue (13x19cm)

34

13. Frank Williams – Spring Morning at Westminster (18x10cm)

14. Trevor Jones – Evening in Mudeford (14x15cm)

15. Trevor Jones – The White Cottage (17x12cm)

16. Trevor Jones – Landscape (18x14cm)

17. Trevor Jones – Evening (14x12cm)

18. Trevor Jones – Architectural Study (11x13cm)

19. Gilbert Hooper – A Corner of Old England (17x27cm)

20. Gilbert Hooper – November Morning (17x26cm)

21. Gilbert Hooper – Cauldron (14x23cm)

43

22. Gilbert Hooper – Tranquillity (15x23cm)

23. Gilbert Hooper – The Trough (13x22cm)

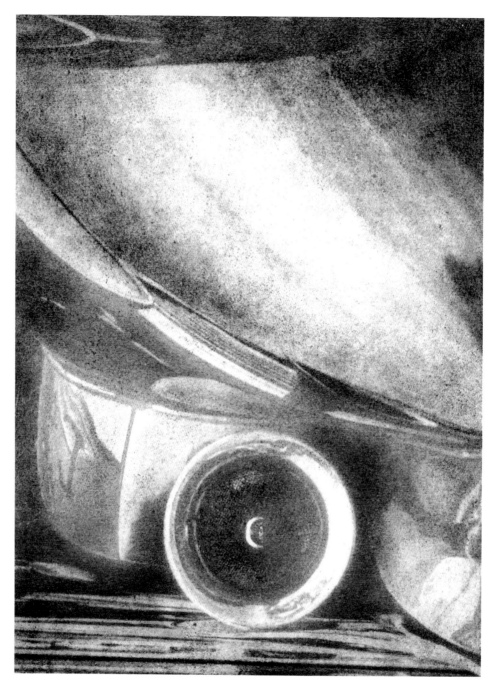

24. Maija McDougal – On the Edge of Abstract 1 (18x24cm)

25. Maija McDougal – Mask (24x24cm)

47

26. Maija McDougal – On the Edge of Abstract 2 (18x25cm)

27. Maija McDougal – Tate Gallery (18x26cm)

28. Maija McDougal –Babushka (22x16cm)

29. Derek Ashman – Lonely Boat (12x17cm)

30. Derek Ashman – Penhow Castle (12x17cm)

31. Derek Ashman – Riverside Cottage (12x17cm)

32. Ray Beaumont – Rhigos Road, Rhonda (17x12cm)

33. Ray Beaumont – Old Barn (18x14cm)

34. Leonard Dorricott – The Light of the World (23x33cm)

35. Leonard Dorricott – Parabolic Shadow (23x33cm)

36. Leonard Dorricott – Encounter (19x26cm)

37. David Francis – French Doorway (16x21cm)

38. David Francis – Dummy (21x15cm)

39. David Francis – Chateau Beynac (30x26cm)

40. Kenneth Hill – Penygarn (13x19cm)

41. Kenneth Hill – Carreg Cennen Castle (18x14cm)

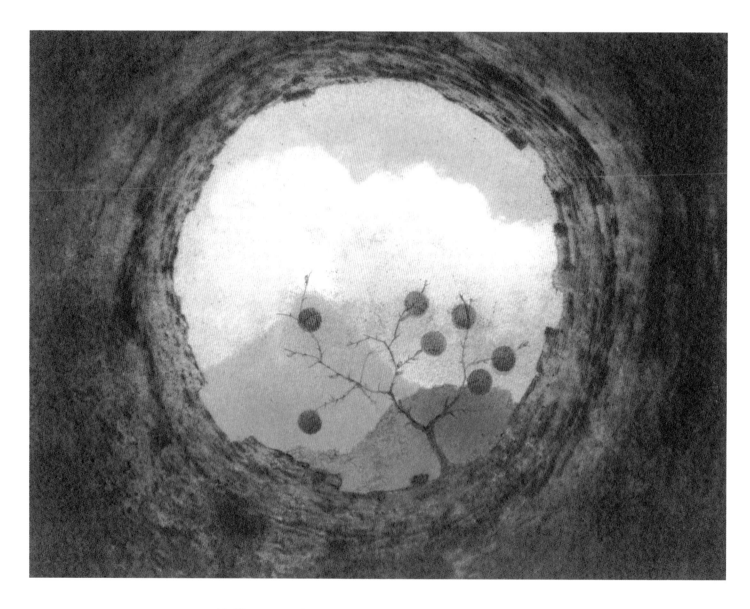

42. Kenneth Hill – The Land of the Demon (18x16cm)

43. Brian Iddon – Ship Study (12x19cm)

44. Brian Iddon – Woodyard, Eastnor (12x20cm)

45. Brian Iddon – Aber Ogwen, Bangor (14x19cm)

46. Elizabeth Kemp – Landscape No. 1 (37x26cm)

47. Elizabeth Kemp – Landscape No. 2 (32x24cm)

48. Elizabeth Kemp – Landscape No. 3 (32x24cm)

49. David Leslie – Old Calton Burying Ground (13x20cm)

71

50. David Leslie – Guardian (19x13cm)

51. David Leslie – Kissing Gate (19x13cm)

52. Peter Potter – Baskets (22x17cm)

53. Peter Potter – Thurn Windmill (23x21cm)

54. Peter Potter – Chassee (13x16cm)

55. Geoffrey Preece – Determination (19x14cm)

56. Geoffrey Preece – Truro City (15x20cm)

57. Geoffrey Preece – Taplow Station (21x16cm)

58. Vivienne Preece – Creperie (14x19cm)

59. Vivienne Preece – Watering Can and Barrow (14x19cm)

60. Vivienne Preece – Milk Churn (14x19cm)

61. Kenrick Roff – Dandelions (21x16cm)

62. Kenrick Roff – Barges off Southend (26x17cm)

63. Kenrick Roff – Plumb (14x20cm)

64. Margaret Sheppard – Spheres (19x14cm)

65. Margaret Sheppard – Wheel (19x14cm)

66. Margaret Sheppard – Lone Rider (26x14cm)

67. Allan Smith – Loch Ard (19x15cm)

68. Allan Smith – The Curling Pond (14x20cm)

69. Allan Smith – Loch Morar (19x14cm)

70. Keith Spencer – Lady from Senegal (19x28cm)

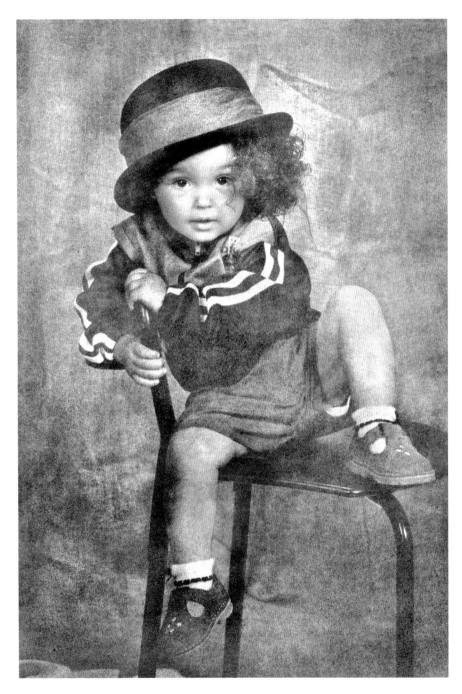

71. Keith Spencer – Mighty Atom (20x29cm)

72. Keith Spencer – Caroline (20x24cm)

73. David Symonds – The Old Haberdashery Shop (21x17cm)

95

74. David Symonds – Duel (22x16cm)

75. David Symonds – Gone (18x22cm)

76. Kirk Toft – Whitley Gazebo (Transfer, 11x13cm)

77. Kirk Toft – Winter, Stamford Bridge (17x17cm)

78. Kirk Toft – Howarth (17x18cm)

79. Gene Laughter – Richmond, Virginia, USA (20x17cm)

80. Gene Laughter – Capel-y-Fin (16x22cm)

81. Gene Laughter – Man with Guitar (16x19cm)

82. George Parr – Magestic Sweep (32x20cm)

83. Anthony Gigg – They Have Their Own Beauty (19x12cm)

84. Cal Humphrey – A Portrait (29x38cm)

85. Albert Barraclough – Threshing (36x29cm)

86. Tom Shipley – The Long Shadow (15x20cm)

87. Tom Shipley – High Sea, Brighton (19x14cm)

88. Gordon Strugnell – Serenity (15x9cm)

89. J. A. Harvey – December Morning (20x13cm)

90. Edward Hirst – Haze in the City (16x18cm)

91. Owen Foster – Morning Sunshine (24x34cm)

92. Owen Foster – Fish Street, Shrewsbury (30x32cm)

93. Georgia Procter-Gregg – Pond Art (20x36cm)

94. Georgia Procter-Gregg – Tree Forms (24x33cm)

95. Helen James – Winter (15x22cm)

96. Helen James – Sanctuary (16x24cm)

97. Joan Moignard – Pennine Way (Transfer, 20x16cm)

98. Horace Brooks – Parish Church, Wolsingham (19x20cm)

99. Percy Deal – Corner of a Field (25x16cm)

100. T. G. W. Thompson – Perspective (20x16cm)

Biographies

Derek Ashman *LRPS*

In 1970 I started photography as a hobby, but over the next 25 years acquired qualifications to branch into professional work which has embraced teaching, employment as a photographic technician and freelance work.   All my activities and work have centred around Swansea, where I live.

It was in the 1990's, after seeing demonstrations by two well known Welsh bromoilists, Gilbert Hooper and Kenneth Hill, I thought I would like to do the process myself.

Being interested in all the old photographic printing processes, I made a start by attending a Bromoil workshop at NEC, Birmingham, organised by the Bromoil Circle and in 1997 I became a member of the society.

I now conduct talks and workshops on the process and have taken part in numerous exhibitions in Wales, including personal shows at the Swansea Museum in 1999 and in 2002 at Det Logistics Llanelli.

Ray Beaumont

A Kodak Brownie 127 camera was my starting point in photography at the age of seven. These days I have a varied collection of cameras and work in my own fully equipped studio.

My personal photography is all film based. I like to produce monochrome prints, cyanotypes, and gum bichromates. I have been playing with the Bromoil Process on and off for a few years, but have recently decided to make a concerted effort to improve my technique and picture quality.

I am currently teaching photography and with some European funding have set up a darkroom. The classes have gone well culminating in small exhibitions embracing monochrome film photography as well as digital imaging.

Leonard W. Dorricott

I first became interested in photography in 1943 during my service as a navigator in R.A.F. Bomber Command. From 1948 to 1964 I used home-made enlargers to produce half-plate monochrome prints for my own interest.

In 1966 I joined Lincoln Camera Club. Over the next year or two, I saw examples of Bromoils by several members of the club. I was so impressed that I took up the challenge and produced my first bromoil in 1973.   By 1975 I had started to give Bromoil demonstrations to clubs in the North East Midlands Photographic Federation and the Lincolnshire Photographic Association. In the same year, conducting a demonstration at the N.E.M.P. Symposium, I met the renowned bromoilist Georgia Procter-Gregg, a member of the Bromoil Circle. I was invited to join the Circle. It was a great honour and I have continued to enjoy my membership ever since.

Nowadays I restrict my club photography to large Bromoils for club competitions and external exhibitions, with some success, leaving digital photography to the younger generation.

David Francis

My first experiment in photography was in 1940 at the age of seven. Seven years later it became a serious hobby when a photographic club was set up at my secondary school in 1947. Materials were scarce and the equipment primitive, but that did not deter me from progress.

At the local library I had access to the "Amateur Photographer" and I fell in love with the reproductions of bromoils, particularly of silver birch trees.

The equipment I used in the early days was plate cameras of all sizes, a favourite being Thornton-Pickard Ruby Reflex.

Years later I attended a Bromoil workshop conducted by the members of the Bromoil Circle. I was invited to join it and eventually appointed Exhibition Officer. In 2000 I became Hon. Secretary of the Society taking very keen interest in promoting the interests of the Circle and the Bromoil process generally.

Alas, as yet I have not bromoiled a silver birch tree!

Kenneth Hill *FRPS*

The first time I saw a Bromoil print was in 1972 by the late Gilbert R. Hooper, at the Welsh Photographic Salon in Bridgend. I was immediately attracted by the appearance of this image which evoked a romantic past and inspired me to find out more about this photographic printing process.

Bromoils possess an inherent nostalgia for a forgotten world of stillness and repose and one in which the human figure gives a feeling of romance to the landscape. It was a memorable day for me, November 20th 1975, when I created my very first Bromoil, alas, far from being technically a perfect print.

Unwilling to give up my ambition to produce quality Bromoils, in the style of the Edwardian period,

I persisted and in 1990 I was fortunate enough to acquire an authentic Bromoil printing press which has enabled me to produce Bromoil Transfer prints.

Gilbert R. Hooper *FRPS*

It was October 1948 when my interest in serious amateur photography was born. At the time an exhibition was held in the local Swansea Club which I visited and saw what I thought were the most wonderful photographs. I made it my business to join the club. Picked everybody's brains. Bought a second hand Voigtlander Bessa camera. Built a rather "Heath Robinson" enlarger, but it worked. My main interest was Tabletop photography. The reason being that I found I had more control over the final results.

I was introduced to the Bromoil process by the late Evan Evans, who gave a demonstration at the club. I immediately saw the vast control of the final image available by the process and became completely sold on it. From then on I had very little interest in any other method of producing prints.

In 1971 I gained my Royal Photographic Society's Associate distinction in the process. I was then invited to join the Bromoil Circle, a band of about a dozen dedicated bromoil workers determined to keep the process alive. In 1981 I was granted Fellowship by the RPS. I consider that one of my greatest achievements is that I was awarded the Ronald Jonas Landscape trophy by the UPP with a bromoil print.

My interest in the Bromoil process lies in the fact that it offers so much control in the making of a picture. The camera allows to *Take,* but the process allows to *Make* pictures.

(An abridged extract from an article Gilbert Hooper had submitted to the RPS Pictorial Group magazine "Visual Art" in 1997)

Brian Iddon *LRPS*

My interest in the Bromoil Process was started by the late Helen James ARPS and Gilbert Hooper FRPS, past President of the Bromoil Circle, who visited my camera club in Menai Bridge, Anglesey, to do a demonstration. That was back in 1985 when my main interest in photography was monochrome printing.

The demonstration highlighted to me the beauty of a Bromoil image, full of quality and detail and very individualistic. Having an interest in the old photographic processes and early photography in general, I was immediately taken by the Bromoil Process.

The expert teaching of both Helen James and Gilbert Hooper taught me the technical control of how to produce a Bromoil image. I feel very privileged to have been inspired and tutored by these two outstanding masters of the Art of Bromoil.

I still work in the darkroom doing monochrome printing, bromoiling, some alt. processes and experimenting with various chemicals and papers.

Elizabeth Kemp

After three years studying photography, I spent two years in my darkroom practising all the skills learned in the various branches of photography, including the alternative printing processes.

However, I had not studied the Bromoil technique, but came across it for the first time in the publication "Photo Art International". I found the displayed Bromoil images fascinating.

A workshop was to be held at the RPS in Bath. I enrolled and watched with great interest Gilbert Hooper, the tutor, demonstrating. It was the little back room in the Octagon at Bath where I produced my first Bromoil print. From there on I was hooked.

There were many waste bins full of attempts to start with. Nothing worthwhile comes easily, but eventually the necessary skills are mastered and with this comes the control of the image you are visualising.

Gene Laughter *Hon Member of BCGB*

After retiring I turned to photography as a serious hobby around 1993. I became interested in the Bromoil Process after seeing Bromoil reproductions in books and magazines. Thus began a long journey of research and learning.

In the early days, unfortunately, I was working in somewhat of a vacuum. Guiding information was gathered mainly from the literature I had collected and eventually by attending Bromoil workshops conducted, alas, in a very strict traditionalists' manner.

The direction of my Bromoil work, however, is to break away and utilise the process with today's imagery.

In 1996 I established contact with the B.C. of G.B. The following year and in 1998 I visited Britain to participate in the Society's meetings. Close links were established and I was awarded Honorary membership of the Circle.

In 1996, upon returning to the States, I began writing a working manual covering my methods of the process. It resulted, a year later, 1997, in the publication of "Bromoil 101", a plain English working manual and users' guide for beginners.

Over the years I have conducted numerous workshops, demos, organised meetings, "Hopperfests" and participated in exhibitions throughout the U.S.A, all with the aim of introducing Americans, interested in the alternative photographic printing processes, to the Art of Bromoil.

David Leslie

Born Edinburgh 1933, educated at George Heriot's School. After National Service, I joined what is now National Air Traffic Services and spent most of my working life at the Scottish and Oceanic Air Traffic Control Centre at Prestwick, Ayrshire. On retirement I returned to Edinburgh in 1993.

Mainly involved in black and white photography, my interest in the Bromoil Process was triggered by seeing the image "December Morning" by Kirk Toft, a member of the Bromoil Circle of Great Britain, in the (now defunct) Creative Monochrome yearbook "Best of Friends", No. 5. I became a member of the Circle in October 2004.

Maija McDougal *FRPS*

My serious interest and involvement in photography began in the late 1970's. After attending college courses in London, I took, as an amateur, the usual steps and joined a number of photographic societies. My activities there embraced transparency work, colour and monochrome printing.

Very soon my interests were channelled towards the early photographic printing processes, particularly Gum Bichromate, and Bromoil. By 1985, having received instructions from the distinguished Welsh bromoilist, Gilbert Hooper, the Bromoil Process replaced all previous photographic activities.

In 1985 I joined the Bromoil Circle of Great Britain and for 11 years acted as its secretary. In 2000 I was elected by the members to become the 6th President of the Society.

In 1989 I was awarded The Royal Photographic Society's Associateship distinction and Felloship in 1997, after submitting panels of Bromoil prints on both occasions.

Over the years I have taken part in many exhibitions with Bromoil prints and transfers and have conducted numerous demonstrations and workshops in England, France, The Netherlands, US, Australia and Latvia, the country of my birth.

Bromoiling was taken up just as a pastime hobby to start with. However, my involvement in the affairs of the Circle during the 22 years of membership did become a full time, greatly rewarding and absorbing, occupation.

Peter Potter *LRPS*

Around the mid' 80s I began matters photographic by joining my local camera club, a great place for learning. Time marched on and I became known as the "technical one" - the artistic side of things took just a bit longer. In due course I became a big fish in a small pond. It was time for a move to a bigger pond. I joined the Royal Photographic Society and vanished!

Then resurfaced through obtaining my Licentiate-ship award.

The RPS magazine ran details regarding a Bromoil course. The process had always been one of my ambitions, so a hopeful request for a place on the course was posted. Unfortunately it was fully booked and I was placed on the waiting list for the next one. When it arrived I had a great day and joined the Circle. Next stage was to see me consuming masses of paper in order to produce some indifferent Bromoils. Never one to give up without a fight, I found the answer to my troubles. I was up and running with evident progress and enjoying my time with the Circle from whom much help has been gleaned.

Vivienne Preece
Geoffrey Preece

Our involvement in bromoiling began when, at a Bristol Camera Fair in the early 90s, the Bromoil Circle was giving a demonstration which caught our attention and interest. Previously Vivienne's interest in photography, which started in 1960 with the purchase of a Voigtlander Vito BL, had been from the point of view of taking holiday and family photographs. Mine (Geoffrey) was rather more involved. It started in 1955 whilst serving in the army in Cyprus. A local photographer taught us the rudiments and the fascination with all things photographic began. Since those days I have never been without a darkroom. In 1999 I was fortunate in having a book published with over 400 of my black and white photographs, the subject being motor bikes. In the 80s we became interested in early photography, both equipment and images.

Our interest in the Bromoil process was mutual and after seeing some more demonstrations, the necessary materials were obtained and practice started. After about two years we joined the Circle. We were fortunate in that we had some wonderful tutors during our learning period, all members of the Bromoil Circle, without whose help we would have given up long ago. A growing fascination with the transfer process and the absence of transfer presses on the market saw us manufacture our own to a design by the Belgian bromoilist, Rene Smets.

Kenrick Roff *ARPS*

I was born in 1921 and my first "dabble in photography" was as a child of 6 years only by bending the bellows mechanism of my father's Kodak folding camera. Ten years later, with the same camera, now repaired, I was photographing the shipping at the Thames Estuary. The resulting snapshots of the Thames barges particularly fascinated me.

During my WW2 Service in New Delhi, I was able to buy a second hand twin-lens reflex camera and photography became my principal leisure activity. In 1951 I lived in Lincoln and joined the local Camera Club whose members helped me to learn about exhibition photography. I had also joined a photographic postal group based in Lincolnshire. A member of this group introduced me to the beauty of Bromoil work and tutored me in the process.

After treating myself to my first Leica camera, I joined the Leica Postal Portfolio group and won a few trophies in their Annual Exhibitions with my Bromoil work. This brought me in contact with the Bromoil Circle of Great Britain who took me in as a member some years ago.

I am still fascinated by Thames Barges and other sailing crafts and can be seen photographing them when I have the opportunity.

Margaret Sheppard

My first recollection of photography was at the age of 12 when my father bought me a Coronet plastic camera. We took photos and roughly developed and printed them in the bathroom. The results were poor, but it was magical to see the prints "come up" in the developer. At the age of 21 my husband bought me a Mamiya SLR. For the next 30 years I produced high contrast black and white prints using various cameras, but finally settling with Leicas.

Other interests I share with my husband are Stereoscopic photography and camera collecting. We are members of Stereoscopic Society, Photographic Collectors Club International and Leica Postal Portfolios.

I had vaguely heard of Bromoils some 10 years ago. Then through reading a little on the subject and seeing some demonstrations by the members of the Bromoil Circle of Great Britain, I became seriously interested in this branch of photography. I joined the Circle and have been actively participating in all its activities, taking part in exhibitions, workshops, demonstrations and the day to day running of the Society. Bromoiling is not an easy task, but when a print is successful it is a very satisfying and rewarding pastime.

Allan Smith

My interest in Photography began during the years I attended the Glasgow School of Art (1950-1955), when I had also purchased a second hand Leica 3B camera. I then joined the Glasgow and West Scotland photographic club and later Leica Postal Portfolios. I am still a member of the latter as well as the Scottish Photographic Circle.

My interest in Bromoil started in Circle 7 of the Leica Postal Portfolios with the excellent Bromoil prints submitted by Richard Taylor, one of its members. His influence and help enabled me to get started.

A visit to Callender House Museum in Falkirk, where the Bromoil Circle of Great Britain had an exhibition, interested me to make further enquiries regarding membership. I was delighted to be accepted and find the fascination of bromoiling to be an ongoing learning process. The members of the Circle have been most helpful with hints and tips and imparting their experience and knowledge.

Keith Spencer *FRPS*

Following my full time education at Keighley School of Art & Crafts, and a further six years part time training there, I was always intrigued with artistic subjects. I think it was automatic that I moved to photography and it's associated crafts. I took a photography course at Keighley Technical College, and I was hooked.

Next I joined the Royal Photographic Society and gained the following distinctions: Licentiateship, Associateship and Fellowship.

I was introduced to the Bromoil Process by Tom Shipley, a past Hon. Secretary of the Bromoil Circle of Great Britain. It was he who first demonstrated the process to me and I eventually became a member of the Society. I have been President of the Keighley & District Photographic Society on three occasions.

I am exceedingly grateful to past and present members of the Circle for their guidance and encouragement, most notably the late Gilbert Hooper.

David Symonds *FRPS*

I was born in Birmingham, England in 1948 and live now in Scotland working as a lighting designer on a semi-retired basis.

Until 1984 my main interest in the arts was water colour painting. Involvement in photography was accidental, when I borrowed an SLR camera to take pictures of my daughter and became hooked. Initially I created surreal manipulated images in both transparencies and monochrome prints.

In April 1991 I gained two ARPS distinctions and Fellowship followed 6 months later with a panel of hand coloured monochrome prints. In 1992 I received the AIFPA distinction, followed by EFIPA in 1995.

My interest in Bromoil was also accidental. In 1999, whilst judging a photographic exhibition in Coventry, there were a number of Bromoil entries, which took my eye. They were like no other print I had seen. The grain, ink, paper and texture all conspired to produce an effect that was inspiring. After further investigation

I made contact with the Bromoil Circle and eventually became a member.

My current photographic interests range from Digital imaging at one end of the spectrum, to Bromoil printing at the other. I now combine the two by making digital contact negatives on the computer, which replace the conventional film negative. From there conventional Bromoil techniques are used to produce the final image.

Kirk Toft *LRPS*

I have had a long interest in Victorian and Pre-Raphaelite paintings which led me to try and create my own images of rustic scenes. However, instead of painting, I began to experiment with photography. After coming across illustrations which had the appearance of etchings and mezzotints, I discovered they were actually reproductions of Bromoil and Oil prints. At this point I decided to try my hand at these processes. I felt these would compliment the style of images I liked and so began my "love affair" with Bromoil.

There followed two years of experimentation, failure after failure, and I knew of no-one who could advise. The old publications I came across did not offer a great deal of help.

I had recently joined the Royal Photographic Society, which was more helpful, and who informed me that a workshop on the Bromoil process was to be held in Bradford at, what used to be called, The National Museum of Photography, Film and Television. It was run by the Bromoil Circle of Great Britain. Not long afterwards I became a member of the Circle.

Besides having created many images in the Bromoil process, I am working with allied pigment processes such as Oleobrom (the only known worker in the U.K.) and just two years ago have started to work in Rawlings Oil-Process, which was the predecessor of Bromoil. I now work exclusively in the transfer technique.

I live and work in West Yorkshire and have delivered lectures and demonstrations regularly throughout this region as well as other parts of Great Britain. Many of my images have been widely exhibited and published in books and magazines.

Bibliography

1. Brookes A. E., My Approach to Bromoil, The Photographic Journal, R.P.S., August 1960
2. Cox B. & Tilney F. C., Tracts: for Pictorial Photographers, No3 The Art of Pigmenting, 1924
3. Crawford William, The Keeper of Light, Morgan and Morgan, 1979
4. Fielding Dennis, The Alchemists Manual, Self publication
5. Fielding Dennis, Pigment Printing, Darkroom User, Issue No30 – 1997
6. Gabriel L. G., Bromoil and Transfer a Practical Manual, Pitman & Sons, 1930
7. Hawkins G. L., Pigment Printing, Henry Greenwood & Co, 1933
8. Hawkins G. L., The Bromaloid Process and Bromaloid Inks, Hawkins, 1951
9. Hooper Gilbert R., An Introduction to Bromoil, Bromoil Circle of Great Britain, 1997
10. Judge F. & Tilney F. C., Tracts: for Pictorial Photographers, No2 Oil, Bromoil & Transfer, Greenwood and Co, 1923
11. Laughter Gene, Bromoil 101, Self publication, 1997, also B.C. of G.B.
12. Lewis David, The Art of Bromoil & Transfer, Self publication, 1995
13. Mayer Dr E., Bromoil Printing and Bromoil Transfer, American Photographic Publishing Co, 1913/1923
14. Mayer Dr E., A Manual of Bromoil and Transfer, American Photographic Publishing Co, 1927
15. Nadeau Luis, History and Practice of Oil & Bromoil Printing, Self publication, 1993
16. Misonne Leonard, How I make my Oil Prints, The American Annual of Photography, 1937
17. Mortimer F. J. & Coulthurst S. L., The Oil and Bromoil Processes, Hazell, Watson & Viney, 1912
18. Partington Chas. H., Bromoil and Bromoil Transfer, The Complete Photographer, Issues No 8 & 9
19. Procter-Gregg Georgia, My Way with the Bromoil Process, R.P.S. Pictorial Group Journal, 1978
20. Reed Martin & Jonas Sarah, Silver Gelatine, Working Books Ltd., 1995
21. Sanderson Andrew, Hand Colouring & Alternative Darkroom Processes, Roto Vision, 2002
22. Symes C. J., Perfection in the Pigment processes, handbook No3, The New Photographer Ltd, 1924
23. Whalley G. E., Bromoil and Transfer, Fountain Press, 1961
24. Watkins Derek, Bromoil – A Foundation Course, Photographer's Institute Press, 2006